SOUTHWEST USA

SOUTHWEST USA

80 color photographs by Gerd Kittel

Introduction by Peggy Larson

THAMES AND HUDSON

For Inke

For help and support I would like to thank Stanley Baron,
Suzanne Crayson, Eberhard Hinkel, Wolfgang Keller, Ralph
Keller, Werner Kittel, Dick Rautenberg, Martin Squires,
Ingeborg Welther. I am also indebted to the firm
Lufthansa A.G.

Photographs and captions © 1986 Thames and Hudson Ltd, London

Text © 1986 Peggy Larson

First published in the United States in 1986 by
Thames and Hudson Inc.,
500 Fifth Avenue, New York, New York 10110

Library of Congress Catalog Card Number 86-50495

Printed and bound in Japan

Contents

Introduction

Southwest USA: a unique and spectacular stage, across which have marched, ridden and trudged some of the most diverse cultures and characters gathered in one area in the last four and a half centuries.

Scenes range from short grass plains, through mountains, plateaus, and river valleys, to a variety of deserts. The region is immense, the vista often limited only by the spectator's powers of vision, the routes across the land traditionally tortuous, and the general overriding climatic factor that of aridity.

The cast has ranged from Indian tribes, savage and warlike or pacific, to Spanish *conquistadóres*, often brutal in their behavior, trailed by priests, *mestizos*, and Indian slaves, Mexican land grant holders, indigent farmers and herders, prospectors, soldiers, and officials, to early Anglo-American invaders, in general no less brutal or avaricious than the Spanish conquerors who preceded them—and, finally, to today's multi-ethnic masses who are drawn to the land for its economic opportunities, climate, and beauty.

The "plot" until now has exhibited continuing conflict between man and the environment, between cultures, and not infrequently between individuals. The Spanish promoted *reducción* of the people and the land. In many ways they and those who eventually followed them were successful. But the land itself exerted its own *reducción* against the human species which invaded it. Each, land and people, has modified the other. For perhaps as many as fifteen millennia the environment strongly controlled and molded the human invaders. In the last century and a half, however, man has been, and increasingly will be, the greater modifier—subduing, reducing, and reshaping, to the diminishment of its inherent aesthetics, this harsh, beautiful, and delicate land.

A line, visible only on maps, marks the beginning of the American West. This is the hundredth meridian, slicing through western North and South Dakota, Nebraska, Kansas, Oklahoma, and Texas. Roughly coincidental with it is the western limit of the great plains' annual average rainfall of twenty or more inches. To the west, rainfall levels generally decrease, the land builds toward the Rocky Mountains, agriculture without irrigation is risky or impossible, short grass prairie is the virgin norm. Then, stretching westward from the Rockies to the Sierra Nevada and related mountain ranges, is a vast area that varies from semi-arid, to arid, to extremely arid, and is marked by numerous lesser mountain ranges and plateaus.

As a portion of this West, the Southwest encompasses extreme western Texas and Oklahoma, southwestern Colorado, southern Utah and Nevada, southeastern California, and all of New Mexico and Arizona, the heartland of the Southwest. Mountain "islands" rise within this area and often receive bountiful moisture; mighty rivers, such as the Colorado and Rio Grande, slice through it, transporting great quantities of water largely derived from outside it. But overall, the common characteristic of the entire area is aridity.

The American Southwest flows uninterrupted into Mexico's adjacent Northwest, and shares with it two major deserts. The Chihuahuan lies primarily in Mexico, but portions of it extend along both sides of the great bend area of the Rio Grande in Texas, and amoeba-like extensions flow into southern New Mexico, reaching north almost to Albuquerque, and into extreme southeastern Arizona. Desert grasslands extend northward and westward from the Chihuahuan, across the low elevations of the southern Continental Divide in western New Mexico and eastern Arizona. The grasslands abut mountain ranges to the north and in places to the west; in others they meet the Sonoran Desert—a vast, rough horseshoe encircling the head of the Gulf of California, its legs extending down over much of Mexico's Baja California peninsula and mainland state of Sonora.

Adjoining the northwestern border of the Sonoran is the Mohave Desert, stretching into southeastern California and southern Nevada, and joined on the north to the Great Basin Desert. Most of the latter—which is colder and higher than the Sonoran—lies north of the limits of the Southwest, but portions of it extend into the Colorado Plateau area of Utah and northern Arizona.

The hottest, driest, and lowest area in the United States is located not far from the head of the Gulf of California. From the Gulf a low trough extends northward; in its more northern portion in the Mohave Desert lies Death Valley, where at Badwater the lowest point in the Western Hemisphere occurs, 282 feet below sea level. The world's second highest maximum temperature, 134° F., has been recorded in the Valley. In one study, the average daily maximum air temperature for the month of July was 120.1° F.; ground-surface temperatures of 190° F. were recorded, as were humidity levels as low as 3 per cent. In Death Valley the sun shines for 90 per cent of daylight hours. In the low-lying desert areas between the Gulf and Death Valley, as at Yuma, Arizona, located along the Colorado River, periods of ninety consecutive days with maximum temperatures of 100°F. or higher are not exceptional.

The Valley holds the record low annual precipitation rate for the United States: 1.6 inches. This is an average; some sites remain without precipitation for extended periods. In Death Valley, on average, in two years out of every fifty, no rainfall is recorded. Bagdad, in the Mohave, is the US record holder for the longest period without measurable rainfall: 767 days. Temperature is a function of both latitude and altitude; as one moves north and east from the desert hub near the Gulf, the land gradually rises, precipitation increases, and maximum temperatures are not so extreme.

In terms of physical geography, the southwestern deserts lie in the Basin and Range Province—so called because the landscape consists primarily of large basins dotted with intervening mountain ranges. In southern Utah, northern Arizona, southwestern Colorado, and northwestern New Mexico, the Basin and Range Province gives way to the Colorado Plateau Province. This covers approximately 130,000 square miles, most of which lies at elevations of 5000 or more feet. Approximately a quarter of the area receives less than ten inches of annual precipitation, much of it snow. The topography consists of layers of colorful sedimentary rocks which have been uplifted, eroded by wind and water, and deeply incised by streams, resulting in magnificent canyons, mesas, cliffs, gorges, badlands, and a vast array of amazing buttes, spires, arches, pinnacles, domes, knobs, bridges, columns, and similar forms.

Ecologically, the Southwest can be categorized according to life zones. The low-lying deserts are classified in the lower Sonoran life zone, characterized by desert vegetation. The plateau area is considered Upper Sonoran, which often supports a desert grassland, desert scrub, or a juniper-piñyon woodland. These two zones predominate, but where higher elevations or mountains rise above them, others, increasingly cooler and wetter, are encountered. In the Plateau area particularly, numerous mountains attain high elevations, many exceeding 11,000 feet. Life zones, in order of elevation, include the Transition with pine forests; the Canadian with fir forests; the Hudsonian with spruce and alpine firs; and finally the Arctic-Alpine with low-growing arctic plants above timberline.

Much of the Southwest, particularly the deserts, imposes stringent conditions upon the plants and animals attempting to live there: low and irregular precipitation patterns; low humidity; prolonged high temperatures; extreme daily and annual temperature fluctuations; long hours of sunlight; erosion of the predominantly barren ground surface by water and winds; and soils low in humus and high in minerals. Solutions to these conditions have produced some of the most interesting and highly adapted plant and animal species in the world, which contribute to the distinctive Southwest landscape.

Some plants take avoiding action from the challenge of aridity, such as those that exist only where water supplies are dependable: cottonwood trees along streams issuing from the higher mountains, mesquite bosques along intermittently flowing desert rivers, or palm trees around one of the rare oases. Seeds of annual plants may lie dormant, sometimes for years, but rapidly germinate, flower, and seed once more when favorable conditions briefly prevail, forming the brilliant blankets of wildflowers for which the deserts are famous.

Other plants—the perennials known as xerophytes—establish roots and face the arid conditions head-on, having adapted physiologically and/or morphologically to their environment. These include the saguaro cacti which dominate the rocky slopes, sometimes reaching fifty feet in height, ten tons in weight and some specimens known to be a hundred years old; innocuous, drought-resistant creosote bushes, redolent after a summer shower; the bunched wands of red-tipped, spined ocotillo; rosettes of fleshy-leaved agaves, their roasted hearts a favorite Indian food; stands of yuccas, of which one impressive species, the Joshua Tree, beckoned the Mormon explorers onward; vast stands of short-statured piñyon and juniper trees marching across a red rock landscape; sagebrush covering basins and hills, as far as the eye can see, with a uniform light gray-green that meets the horizon of a vast blue bowl of sky.

Animals, too, have adjusted to life with aridity, although they, unlike the plants, have the option of mobility. Their adjustments may be behavioral, physiological, or morphological. Many make use of restricted habitats, retreating to shade, burrows underground, or holes in cacti. Their activity may be nocturnal, or they may enter long dormant stages.

Others fly or walk long distances to water holes. Birds soar in light winds in the higher, cooler air levels. One highly adapted species, the kangaroo rat, has an enhanced ability to produce metabolic water, and hence, in conjunction with behavioral adaptations, to derive all the moisture it requires from the dry plant food it consumes.

One member of the animal species, however, possesses few morphological or physiological advantages to combat the Southwest's environmental extremes. This is man, whose primary advantage is his superior brain. He has increasingly used it to devise artificial means by which to adjust behaviorally to the desert, primarily through avoidance: by refrigeration, air conditioning, and the profligate use of water for irrigation, swimming pools and industry. Use of his brain does not necessarily infer that man practices environmental intelligence, for he actually adjusts the desert to himself, rather than adjusting to it. Not so early man, who adapted or perished.

Man entered the Southwest between 12,000 and 15,000 or more years ago. These people were hunters, stalking animals of another geologic era—elephants, camels, horses, sloths, and bison. In southern Arizona they slaughtered them, leaving bones, spear points, stone tools, and remains of fire to be discovered 11,000 years later. The Ice Age came to an end around 10,000 BC, and the big game became extinct, perhaps with man's help. A hunting and gathering people, the Cochise, emerged 2,000 years later and left a record spanning 8,000 years. By 2,000 BC they had received a primitive form of corn from Mexico; by AD 1 squash and beans had been added, and the people were living an agricultural life.

There emerged, by the beginning of the Christian era, several major groups of people in the heartland of the Southwest. The Anasazi (Ancient Ones) lived on the plateau in today's "Four Corners" country where Utah, Colorado, Arizona, and New Mexico meet. They built permanent homes, lived in village arrangements, domesticated the dog and turkey, replaced the atlatl with bow and arrow, developed pottery, flutes, basketry, and wove cotton, robes of feather cloth, and sandals. The climax of Anasazi achievement was reached from about AD 1000 to 1300. By that time they were building huge, multi-storied villages or pueblos, in fine stone masonry, often consisting of hundreds of rooms and complete with plazas and underground kivas. In some instances, although lacking the wheel, they built roads twenty feet wide, radiating 200 miles to connect with outlying areas. These magnificent pueblos were constructed in gigantic rock overhangs in the plateau and canyon country—for example White House ruins in Canyon de Chelly—or in the open, as at Chaco Canyon.

The Hohokam (Vanished) arrived in the Southwest from Mexico around 300 BC and became resident in the desert of southern Arizona. In an arid land they were sedentary farmers who depended upon wise and provident use of available water for their survival. Developing, in the Salt and Gila River Valleys, an intricate system of several hundred miles of hand-excavated canals, which were as much as 30 feet wide and 15 feet deep, the Hohokam became master farmers, raising beans, squash, corn, and cotton. Organization and cooperation were vital to their success; they developed highly organized social, political, and religious systems. They built ball courts, wove beautiful cotton textiles, made pottery, modeled clay, carved stone, developed an acid etching technique for sea shell ornamentation, and imported ideas and items, such as copper bells and live parrots and macaws, from far south in Mexico.

By 1400 the Hohokam and Anasazi had undergone a severe decline in population and culture. Causes can only be conjectured, but a prolonged drought may have been a contributing factor. It is thought that today's Pima and Tohono O'odham (Papago) Indians are modern descendants of the Hohokam. The Anasazi abandoned many of their pueblos and drifted south and east, where a few large centers developed: today's Ácoma, Hopi, Zuñi, and Rio Grande pueblos. In 1540 there were approximately 70 pueblos; today there are less than half that number. The arrival of the nomadic, plundering Apache and Navajo, migrating out of the north sometime after 1500, may have speeded the pueblos' consolidation.

But it was the appearance of Coronado's army on the southern horizon one summer day in 1540 that was permanently to alter life in the Southwest. The soldiers came in search of riches, their credulity based on treasures looted by the Spanish farther south during the previous twenty years.

Fernando Cortés had defeated the powerful Aztecs of Tenochtitlán (Mexico City) in 1521. Twelve years later, the Inca empire of Peru capitulated to the brutal Francisco Pizarro. Rooms of gold and silver, treasures beyond belief, fell to the greedy victors. It was a New World, its limits unknown. Legend and myth fired the Spanish imagination; El Dorado, cities of gold, a nation of Amazons fed their wildest dreams. Their motivations—glory,

God, gold—backed by gullibility and tenacity, as well as lances, crossbows, swords, harquebuses, and horses, brought them far beyond the northern borders of New Spain (to the northern borders of today's Arizona and New Mexico). Coronado's expedition provided an example of Spanish attitudes and actions toward the native people and the land that was to continue, in varying degrees, for the next 300 years.

Francisco Vásquez de Coronado, resplendent in gilded armor, wearing a feather-plumed steel helmet, and riding one of his twenty-three horses, led his party northward. Behind him rode or marched 336 Europeans, most of them cavalrymen, three of their wives, about 1000 Indian men, several of their wives and children, four friars, a herd of 1500 horses and pack animals, and hundreds of goats, sheep, cattle, and hogs. To the west three ships, commanded by Hernando de Alarcón and laden with supplies for the land party, sailed northward to the head of the Sea of Cortez (Gulf of California). The Army marched in search of the fabled Seven Cities of Gold, or Cíbola. The presumed location of the cities had been based on rumors heard by three Spaniards and a black slave who, shipwrecked in Florida in 1528, made their way westward, endured Indian captivity, and in 1536 returned to northern Mexico.

Subsequently the slave, Estéban, was sent with a Franciscan friar, Marcos de Niza, to check out the rumors. Estéban was killed at the Zuñi pueblo of Háwikuh, in northwestern New Mexico, apparently in a disagreement regarding the availability of Indian women. Thereupon the friar, trailing many leagues to the rear, turned and retreated. Unwilling to disappoint those who sent him or to admit he fled precipitately, he reported he had viewed Háwikuh from a nearby hill and it was "larger than the city of Mexico," thereby setting in motion the Coronado entrada.

What an adventure it must have been! By the time Coronado's dusty, tired entourage arrived at the Zuñi pueblos it was considerably diminished in size and was immediately greatly disappointed. A battle ensued with the residents of Háwikuh, during which Coronado suffered wounds from having been struck on his plumed helmet by boulders hurled from the rooftops. Discouraged, but not defeated, Coronado continued to follow the glittering, golden rumors—these offered freely by the Indians who sought the Spaniards' immediate departure. Coronado sent a party to the Hopi pueblos in northeastern Arizona to search. Another group investigated reports of a great river, thereby discovering the Grand Canyon. Yet another, led by Melchior Díaz, departed to contact the supply ships.

To Díaz's dismay, he discovered the Gulf lay far to the west and south. Alarcón had already arrived there, then ascended the Colorado River, perhaps as far as modern Yuma. Unable to make contact with the land party, he had buried letters under a marked tree and departed. Díaz found the messages; suspected a plot among the Yuma Indians; captured, tortured, and killed one, and then several others in the battle that ensued; and soon after died himself, as a result of being accidentally impaled on his own lance.

Back on the plateau, Coronado sent another party eastward under Hernando de Alvarado. This reached the Rio Grande and the Tiguex pueblos, near modern Albuquerque, then moved northward to Taos pueblo. Coronado followed and cleared the residents out of one of the Tiguex pueblos, using it for winter quarters. The conquerors demanded large supplies of food and clothing from the Indians. An Indian woman was raped. The natives objected and fighting ensued. The Spaniards thereupon seized one of the recalcitrant pueblos, destroyed it, and prepared to burn 200 of its inhabitants at the stake. They resisted, and further fighting occurred in which over 100 of the victims were killed and about 70 more escaped, leaving a mere 30 for the burning.

In the spring, following the promising stories of a captive Plains Indian, Coronado's army marched north and east to the central part of Kansas. There, among the huts of the Wichita Indians, the Spaniards faced the ugly truth: in this prairie land there were no mountains, no trees—and no gold. Coronado had the captive liar strangled. The Spaniards returned to Tiguex, where they spent a miserable winter. The previous spring, having frightened away, killed, or taken captive all the residents, they now found no supplies to be commandeered. Also, that winter Coronado was seriously injured in a fall from his horse.

Defeated, ill, reviled by many of his followers, Coronado returned to Mexico to face humiliation, poor health, and, twelve years later, death at the age of forty-four. He had not found the treasure he sought, and had failed to recognize the treasure he discovered.

Following Coronado's return, understandably, there was little Spanish interest in the area he had explored. A few small parties entered New Mexico, including several friars, most of whom died there for their faith, including three from Coronado's Army who chose to remain behind. In 1598, however, a major colonizing party under Juan de Oñate, consisting of 130 families, an additional 300 men, and 7000 head of livestock, followed the Rio Grande northward. Along that river they appropriated a pueblo and its fields, then set

1500 Indians to labor there, without pay, but with benefit of religious conversion. While Oñate was exploring, a party of thirty of the colonists rode to the pueblo of Ácoma and requisitioned food. The Indians lured the Spaniards to the top of their "Sky City," where they killed the leader and twelve soldiers.

Retribution under Oñate was swift and terrible. The Spanish returned with a force of 70, some of whom scaled the precipitous cliffs atop which the pueblo was built. There, room by room, over a three-day period, the Spanish massacred the inhabitants, some of whom chose death by jumping from the cliffs. Reportedly, only 600 of the original population of 6000 lived to surrender. Some were taken as slaves, and all males over twenty-five years of age had one foot cut off. Two years later the same Spanish force burned three pueblos, killed 900 Indians, and took 400 captives. In the meantime Oñate explored into Kansas, then headed west and south, reaching the mouth of the Colorado River. In 1607 Oñate resigned as governor and was recalled by the government. Along the trail known as the Jornada del Muerto (Journey of the Dead) Indians fell upon his party, killing a single member: Oñate's only son.

Oñate's successor moved the colony to a new, more favorable location and in 1609 established the city of Santa Fe. In 1610 the capitol buildings were constructed, and one of these, the Palace of the Governors, remains a focal point of the city and the oldest continuously occupied public building in the United States.

By 1680 the Pueblo Indians were in revolt. Most were virtually slaves, tilling fields and building churches. For the previous five years the Spanish had conducted a campaign to suppress the Pueblos' religious practices. They destroyed the kivas and tried the religious leaders for witchcraft. Three were hanged; more would have been, had not seventy warriors stormed the Palace. One who escaped hanging was Popé, who fled to Taos pueblo, from which he masterminded the Pueblos' attack upon the Spanish.

In August 1680, 400 Spanish citizens were killed, as were 21 of the 32 priests in New Mexico. The besieged moved into the Palace of the Governors, where they held out ten days, killing about 350 Indians, before the attackers blocked the ditch carrying water to the Palace. The Indians allowed the Spanish in the Palace and the general area, 1000 strong, to evacuate New Mexico and, afoot, to trail south to New Spain. The Indians moved into the Palace. They set about destroying all signs of the Spanish, including the mission churches built in the pueblos. Only two escaped destruction: those at Ácoma and Isleta, which remain in use today.

Not for thirteen years did the Spanish settlers return to New Mexico. In 1693 Diego de Vargas led a colonizing party back to Sante Fe. He requested that the Indians move out of the Palace. They resisted. The water ditch trick was employed and the Indians surrendered. The Spanish executed 70 of them, taking 400 more as slaves.

The reconquest was a long and bloody one. The Spaniards were successful, ultimately, but the price exacted was high, for in the next 175 years, in addition to subduing the Pueblos, the Spanish also fought the fierce Apaches, Comanches, Navajos, and Utes—all relative late-comers to the Southwest, but whose reputations were quickly established and whose names struck terror in the other late-comers, the Spanish, Mexicans, and Anglo-Americans.

At this time, the great Central Plateau of Mexico served as the major avenue into New Mexico and northern Arizona, and gradually the coastal plains of the Gulf of California assumed importance as a corridor into southern Arizona. A remarkable Jesuit, Padre Eusebio Francisco Kino, serves as an example of some of the outstanding men who traveled northward along this route, freely distributing faith and good works. Kino entered Pimeriá Alta in 1687 and remained there to convert Pima and Tohono O'odham Indians until his death in 1711. He established missions, introduced seeds and superior farming methods, and promoted husbandry of sheep, cattle, and horses. He was an incessant traveler and map maker, and mortified his flesh as penance to his faith. Most importantly, he liked and respected the Indians, most of whom reciprocated his friendship. The best known of his missions, San Xavier del Bac, is marked by a beautiful mission building constructed after Kino's death.

Mexican settlers and soldiers moved slowly northward in Sonora and Chihuahua, but the Comanches to the east, and the Apaches across northern Mexico and the wide swath of southern New Mexico and Arizona increasingly gained strength and daring. The Mexican government established a line of *presidios*, or garrison towns, from Gulf to Gulf, near the present boundary line. One of these was established at Tubac, approximately forty miles south of San Xavier del Bac. In 1776 this *presidio* was transferred to Tucson, which was built as a walled city. That same year the commander of the Tubac *presidio*, Juan Baustista de

16

Anza, led overland, through the desert to the Pacific coast, a colony of 244 settlers, more than half of them women and children, to establish the mission and *presidio* that were to become San Francisco.

Spain's days of glory in New Spain, long in decline, terminated in revolution in 1821, and resulted in the establishment of the nation of Mexico. Then, as the Mexican forces of General Antonio López de Santa Anna were annihilating 182 defenders of the Alamo in 1836, the citizens of Texas declared it a republic independent of Mexico; in 1845 it was added to the United States. Stirred by Manifest Destiny (the doctrine of inevitable expansion to the West), the United States entered into the Mexican War in 1846. At the war's end, with the Treaty of Guadalupe Hidalgo signed in February 1848, followed by the Gadsden Purchase of 1853, the United States had increased its area by more than a third. Having earlier gained Texas, it now added New Mexico, Arizona, California, Nevada, Utah, half of Colorado and portions of Wyoming, Kansas, and Oklahoma. A mere eight days before signing the Treaty of Guadalupe Hidalgo, and unknown to the signatories, gold had been discovered in California. By that summer, across the newly acquired country, there began a stampede for gold that dimmed even Coronado's quest.

In a single century, the nineteenth, the Southwest was overrun by brash, tough, aggressive, self-confident, and sometimes foolish "Anglos," whose interests frequently clashed with those of the Indians and Mexicans. The latter two also warred against each other, and individual Indian tribes fought one another. Changes were rapid, dramatic and often disastrous. The Apaches, Navajos, and other tribes watched the newcomers with apprehension; particularly after 1848, they observed the numbers of these invaders increase and native unease built to an explosive climax.

The Apaches and Comanches, given the legacy of the horse from Spain, had developed a culture based on the raiding and pillaging of Mexican and Anglo settlers. The Indians, often with the help of unscrupulous Mexican traders, carried on a lively business of capture and trade of children and young women to be used as slaves. These were obtained from Mexican and occasionally Anglo settlements, or from rival Indian tribes.

There was extreme antipathy between the Mexicans and Apaches. Scalp hunting was promoted by the Sonoran government in the 1830s—100 pesos for the hair of an Apache warrior, 50 for a squaw's, and 25 for a child's. Gangs of headhunters—Mexicans, Indians, and renegade Anglos—materialized. Their efforts failed to diminish the Apache problem, but sometimes diminished the number of Mexicans, whose scalps were substituted for Apaches'.

Some of the Apaches maintained an uneasy friendship with the incoming Anglos. However, in 1863, Mangas Coloradas, great chief of the Mimbreños Apaches, was lured into an American prospector-military camp under a flag of truce. Made a prisoner, during the night he was burned on the feet and legs with heated bayonets, then shot and "killed while attempting to escape." There is some doubt that he had any opportunity to try to escape. He was decapitated, his brain weighed for comparison to those of "intelligent" Anglos, and his skull sent East. His followers retaliated.

Cochise was the renowned chief of the Chiricahua Apaches and originally tolerant of Anglos. When in 1860 Apaches from a different group raided an Anglo ranch in southern Arizona and stole a child, US Army Lieutenant George Bascom, recently graduated from West Point and new to the Southwest, accused Cochise's band of the attack. In a meeting where Cochise denied his group's involvement, Bascom attempted to arrest the chief. Cochise escaped, but five of his men were captured. Two of these men were killed while attempting to escape. Three more Apaches were captured, making a total of six. In an approaching wagon train the Apaches killed eight Anglos, and three more were taken captive. Three Anglo friends of Cochise went out to plead with him; they too were taken captive. Cochise suggested trading his six prisoners for the six Apaches held by Bascom. The officer refused. Cochise tortured his six prisoners to death. Bascom hung the six Apaches. A major war destined to cause havoc for the next twenty-five years was thus initiated. It did not end until 1886, when with most of the southwestern Indians of all tribes either dead or confined to reservations, Geronimo and his small band of Apaches surrendered to General Nelson Miles in Skeleton Canyon near the Arizona-Mexico boundary.

From the 1850s onwards, forts were established and manned throughout the Southwest. Surveys for railroads were conducted, and these were eventually constructed. The cattle industry mushroomed; by the 1890s overgrazing in southern Arizona had resulted in permanent scarring of the land. Prospectors swarmed over the dry hills. Southern forces raised the Confederate flag over New Mexico and Arizona during the Civil War; Union forces later regained control.

Big, wild, and poorly governed, the Southwest drew outlaws and opportunists from Mexico, Texas, California, and elsewhere. Every man looked out for himself, sometimes legitimately, sometimes at the expense of others. They were aided by Samuel Colt's invention of the repeating pistol with a revolving cylinder; the six-gun wrote an important section of the history of the Southwest.

In 1878 Ed Schieffelin went prospecting in Apache country in southern Arizona. "All the stone you'll find out there is your tombstone," a friend warned him. Instead he struck a rich lode and named the agglomerating town Tombstone. By 1880 it was a rip-roaring frontier settlement with a US Marshal named Wyatt Earp, who was aided by his three brothers and their friend "Doc" Holliday. An ongoing feud developed between them and a gang of outlaws and rustlers, the Brocius-Clanton-McLowery crowd. The result was the shoot-out at the OK Corral, with further sniping and killing to follow.

New Mexico gave birth to the Lincoln County cattle war of 1878 whose dark star was Billy the Kid. Billy died in 1881 at 21, with at least an equal number of notches on his six-gun. The Sundance Kid and Butch Cassidy hid out in the red rock canyons of southern Utah. Throughout the Southwest there were many similar, lesser-known individuals, who, along with Indians, accidents, and disease helped to fill the Boot Hills and lonely and forgotten cemeteries of the Southwest.

Earlier, in 1858, a small US Government steamboat had sailed far up the Colorado River to the villages of the isolated Mohave Indians. As it chugged along near present Needles, California, a pack train of camels, an experiment of the US Army, reached the river. That same year Mormon missionaries entered the area, and the first major wagon train bearing families came into the Mohave territory. Change was immediate and traumatic.

During the years 1852-1856 these Indians had so little contact with Anglos that they were able to have living with them an Anglo captive, Olive Oatman, a fact not known by American Army officers downstream at Fort Yuma. Originally members of a large party headed for California in 1851, through a series of misjudgments and ill luck Olive's family had been facing starvation and were traveling alone along the Gila River in Arizona when attacked by Yavapai Indians. Six family members—father, pregnant mother, and four siblings—were clubbed to death. Olive, thirteen, and her sister, Mary Ann, eight, were taken captive. After one terrible year of captive life with the Yavapai, they were traded to the Mohave Indians. There they were well-treated, but as a result of famine Mary Ann died. In 1856 Olive was regretfully released by the Mohave. At eighteen, tattooed on her face and arms by the Mohaves, Olive returned to Anglo society.

There she eventually married a banker. Earlier, he had herded cattle to California for sale in the gold fields, and just south of the Arizona border had watched his brother die in an attack by Apaches. Only eight years after Olive's release, changes for the Mohave people had been so catastrophic that their former breechcloth-clad chief traveled in a black suit to Washington, D.C., to appeal to President Lincoln for a reservation for his defeated people. In New York City, smartly dressed, tattooed Olive Oatman sought him out to obtain news of her Indian "family" and friends.

In this century in the Southwest major cities have been built, travel has become simple, the desert is ameliorated by air conditioning, races need not fear one another, horses and six-guns are fewer. The frontier has been tamed and tempered. Yet the roots of this bright land are apparent and pervasive. There remain areas of red rock and desert wilderness. The melodious Spanish language is heard throughout the area. Villages with Hispanic traditions mark out-of-the-way water courses in New Mexico. Indian tribes maintain their own individual cultures and religious observances in the deserts, mountains, and atop the mesas. We have at last learned to appreciate and enjoy one another—our similarities, as well as our distinctive and enriching differences.

Gerd Kittel's photographs superbly demonstrate Southwestern history and the relationships between the land and the inhabitants of the Southwest. He has captured the magnificent scenery. He has pictured man's mark upon the land. Seldom has he photographed man, nor has he needed to do so. In these studies man's imprint has been highlighted by the absence of his image and the presence of his works. Of these, a few only, such as the Indian pueblos and the San Xavier del Bac mission, are inherently beautiful. Kittel, however, has interpreted man's imprint as beautiful, mundane, garish, and ugly, as well as the natural landscapes, through an artist-photographer's eye. The results are outstanding photographic studies from which the viewer derives an expanded perspective, understanding, and appreciation of the unique Southwest USA.

Captions

1	Monument Valley, Arizona
2, 3	Grand Canyon, Arizona
4	Jim Gray's Indian Country, road to Meteor Crater, Winslow, Arizona
5	Saguaro cacti, west of Tucson, Arizona
6, 7	Bryce Canyon, Utah
8, 9	White Sands, New Mexico
10-12	Badlands, between Hanksville and Capitol Reef, Utah
13	Near Silverton, Colorado
14	East of Cortez, Colorado
15	Near Flagstaff, Arizona
16	Indian ruins, Pueblo period, AD 1100-1300, Canyon de Chelly, Arizona
17	Taos pueblo, New Mexico
18	San Luis, Arizona
19	Tesuque pueblo, New Mexico
20	Taos pueblo, New Mexico
21	Isleta pueblo, New Mexico
22	Sunday morning, Globe, Arizona
23	North of Flagstaff, Arizona
24	Badlands, between Hanksville and Capitol Reef, Utah
25	East of Monticello, Utah
26	Movie location, Old Tucson, Arizona
27	Sheriff's office, movie location, Old Tucson, Arizona
28	B & P Tavern, Douglas, Arizona
29	Restaurant, movie location, Old Tucson, Arizona
30	Church interior, Jerome, Arizona
31	Ojo Caliente, New Mexico
32-35	Mountainair, New Mexico
36	Cadillac, near Chiricahua, Arizona
37	Sandstorm, Yuma, Arizona
38, 39	Deming, New Mexico
40	Near Pagosa Springs, Colorado
41	West of Taos, New Mexico
42	Monument Valley, Arizona

THE PLATES

4

9

13

18

27

◁ 26

60

65

◁ 64

79